RE-IN-trospection | Retrospection. Introspection.

Irene Madapati

Presentation by *BookLeaf Publishing*

Web: www.bookleafpub.com

E-mail: info@bookleafpub.com

ISBN: 9789357619882

First edition 2022

DEDICATION

Dedicate this book to my Lord and Saviour Jesus Christ, my husband Krupa (Bunny) and our 6 children that God has blessed us with.

Also to all the thinkers, seekers and fellow introverts.

ACKNOWLEDGEMENT

This book was made possible by God's undeserving grace and reconciling love revealed through Christ on the cross, which have been leading me through different seasons of life through the Holy Spirit. I'm utterly grateful for the adventure filled with richer insights, for heartaches and challenges keeping me more grounded unto the reality of my existence, that has brought the writer in me out to the fore.

The family of my parents, brother and grandparents that were beyond my control; the family of friends and foes that are of my own making; the colleagues and acquaintances that I crossed paths with; the readers and supporters that have planted the seed in me to write a book; the church members and medical professionals that I have interacted with; I owe every single one of them and everyone whom I crossed paths with, for all the learnings, the insights and perspectives gained, and the encouragement.

Much of my inspiration to write happened particularly during the season of motherhood – I couldn't have done this without my precious children - Isaiah Kruthagnya Reddy, Kivah Deenaanya Reddy and Kitrah Dhrithivanya Reddy - their support and understanding, letting me write peacefully esp during the many nights, blessing me with their precious sleep. Finally, the whole reason of doing this is because of my dear husband – Krupakanth Reddy – his persistent faith in me, supporting me, pushing me to not give up, leading me unto correction, covering me in prayers and constantly pointing me to Christ.

PREFACE

To the Reader -

After more than 2 decades of self-journaling, about 15 years of blogging, a few months into micro-blogging and much prompting, I'm utterly grateful and truly humbled to finally get to do this a bit more formally and prayerfully. This is a small collection of my writings over a period introspecting life's moment(s) retrospectively in the context of my faith. I love to muse, write, pen down my thoughts and am passionate about undertaking creative projects. Join in on a musing trip with me one poem a time, enter in!

- The Author

"And whatever you do, do it heartily, as to the Lord and not to men" - Colossians 3:23

More Than Enough

Strong enough to be weak,
Powerful enough to be meek,
Supreme enough to be forgiving and loving
unconditionally,
Royal enough to pay the price with death
on my behalf... willingly!

Valiant enough to defeat
the sting of sin in death so brazenly,
Majestic enough to ascend
back to the place of dwelling originally,
Merciful enough to forgive and embrace anyone
at the feet of the cross...
oh, ever so joyfully!

Guard the Heart!

When Discernment is blurred, the gates are
opened for Confusion
to flood in and the lamp of Wisdom is slowly
eroded...
Lo and behold, A fool is in the making!

But when the Will perseveres to search out the
lost Light,
the warm rays of Understanding respond and
gush enter
to re-kindle the Wisdom and Discernment,
re-building around them the layer of Conscience
with a reverential Fear.

The Will is oft persuaded by the Spirit in the
Heart
unto either Perseverance or Foolishness.

Take guard of the Heart, therefore!

A discerning heart always seeks knowledge

Lord! What is right? What is wrong?
I do not know;
In you I put my trust,
To you alone I bow...

Give me wisdom
Give me strength
while I pursue this journey
of Life, to be a witness of Your kingdom.
All around is arrogance, myth and filth!
O! My heart grieves in pain and agony!

I wish I could fly
high up the sky, into the clouds...
when the world is still asleep,
in search of Your glory
and peace, singing praises of joy all along!
And return to sow the good so I can reap an
eternal harvest!

All is vanity

Lord, grant me a faithful heart
to bear all things in the chart,
grant me the diligence and perseverance
so I do not give up on Your blessed assurance
for I understand that all is vanity
all the trials and prosperity
for the end of man's life is certain
except for Your grace, a living fountain.

A whole new world order

5

Compromising convictions,
Aiding addictions,
Convoluting corrections,
Factualising fictions,
Enforcing expectations,
Permitting perversions.

Truly a new world order.

Intolerance in the name of Tolerance,
Malice in the name of Love,
Disobedience in the name of Rights,
Antagonize in the name of Acceptance,
Vengeance in the name of Justice.

Truly a whole new world order!

Sweet whispers

Sweet whispers of comfort when the heart sinks
in sorrow
Oh the joy rushing from within when it realizes
who holds my tomorrow.

Oh the peace and joy,
I can never elsewhere buy!

Oh the love and grace,
I humbly embrace!

Filthy Rags

If only I can fly away
far far away,
from all the filth of the world,
I think to myself...

Oh but wait!
Could I be carrying it?
somewhere within me deep down buried,
waiting to engulf...

Narrow is The Way

Is this the wrong way?

What does it give away?

And what is on the way?

Or is there another way?

What's the right way?

Oh but isn't there only one way?

A living sacrifice

The reason for the smiles
despite all the uncertainties amidst,
is the hope of our souls
in God's saving grace revealed through Christ.

My heart overflows with gratitude,
How can I ever Thank You Lord!
I can never ever repay Your mercies,
And so I offer You myself a living sacrifice.

Anchor

When I'm anxious and my mind ponders where
am I heading,
I wonder and realize I could never manage this
far without His leading!

Those fleeting moments of loneliness amidst a
cheerful crowd
makes me nostalgic, reminiscing about families
being afar and abroad...
but are precious reminders of my anchor as I
journey to the heavenly abode.

And so although future unknown,
my hope is found in Christ alone.

I wanna be...

I wanna be a star..
to brighten people with its twinkle..!
I wanna be a flower..
to make others happy with its tenderness..!
I wanna be falling snow on the mountains..
to get captured in the eyes of people..!
I wanna be a sweet aroma..
to refresh people with its fragrance..!
I wanna be the food made by Mother..
to make people feel secure with Affection..!
I wanna be a melodious caprice..
to bring people back to their happy moods..!
I wanna be the smile of a cute baby..
to bring back smiles on everyone..!!

I wish I could do so much more…

I wish I could do more...
so much more than what I'm allowed to!

I wish I could just go..
and reach out to comfort,
those grieving and in need of support.

I wish I could just sing..
to the heavy-hearted,
who from the loved ones have parted.

I wish I could just talk..
to make people understand,
and reason, perhaps they re-think about their
stand?

I wish I could just give..
my money and belongings
and all that I have to those suffering.

The chains of the world, these chains of
socio-economic elements,
they grab my feet, clutch my hands, tie my
body!

They engulf like thorns with all the DO's and
DONT's
and cripple me from doing what I so yearn to
do!

Oh! Why is it so difficult these days to love and
care?
No matter what, nothing can stop me from
appealing to my God in prayer.
He is the One who gives me strength
to press on… yes pray is what I will most
definitely do,
for God is love, revealed in Christ and rewarding
where due!

Love

True Love so hard to find
So pure, compassionate, so kind!

So self-less and unconditional,
Oh so joyful so magical!

Melting away the heart with warmth,
words so ostensibly coy beneath...

Only to be expressed through tears
"And can it be, that I'm yours?!"

Joy Within

Where am I currently, at what state precisely?
This journey of introspection stirs me up
more for the joy and love in Christ.
Deep within, I also feel the nudge -
vibrations of guilt sent out from my soul.
But Oh, are You not faithful, Lord, unto us, unto
me?
that You are able to keep me from falling!

Humbling it is to know about my Lord's saints,
inspiring it is to my heart of their commitment.
Oh the joy that my soul is saved and safe,
that my fathers, fore-fathers heeded to Your
saints.

Praise belongs to You, my Creator, Saviour!
My life I surrender, my will, my very all!

Peace

Fill me with Your Love
Let peace fall like snow
I worship you every second
to experience the Love that never ends..!

You're so Gracious
I surrender all my precious
Nothing's comparable to your presence
Oh! What joy and peace I can sense...!

My everything

You are my hope, my everything, my strength...
You are the one who loveth, You are the one
who careth...
Whoever I am!!

You are with me wherever I go..
You make me reap all that I sow.
Without You am nothing at all..

You strengthen me when I am weak..
Your presence surrounds me when I fall sick.
Without You am nothing at all..

I need You...

I am weak, I am lame
Who can rescue me from life's brutal game
Only You, I need You

Oh I am a coward, I am a fool!
The wisest of wise who rules,
I pray to You, I need You

I need You, I need You Lord...
Throughout my journey, as I rise and fall
I love You, I love You
For you loved me first, I surrender my very all.

Sufficient Grace

Draw me closer
when I am a loser
Fill me with your truth and peace
when I am at the peak of success
You are my creator who made me
You are the One to chastise and mould me.

Lord You are sufficient to me
nothing else do I want or wish for
Your grace is enough for me
nothing else I need anymore.

Sweet Fellowship

There's a lot of peace
I feel at ease
cause I'm with God

Showers of blessings
Unforeseen happenings
Fill me with awe, I'm spellbound
Oh! His love is profound

Oh what a comfort!
He gives strength to confront
all my difficulties and agony
His fellowship is a sweet harmony

Glory to You

Glory to You,
I give all the Praise to You...
All the life I live through,
I'll keep on loving You!

I magnify You,
Lord, You are Real and TRUE!
Ever I always do
live my life just for You!

Lord, You are my Salvation,
grant me Your grace
for my sins are only against You!

Make me a new Creation
gift me with Perseverance
to keep the Word of You!!

This is your Day

This is your day,
Plan your way,
Stop the unnecessary sway!

This is your day,
Don't become a prey,
to an abysmal bay!

This is your day,
You ought to pay,
The price for the rules you refuse to obey!

This is your day,
Relinquish the negatives and forever slay,
Make up your mind to always 'TRY'!

This is your day,
Cry out to God and say,
"Be with me, forgive and change me, make my
fears allay"!

This is your day,
Turn not so grey,
Look forward to the hope's ray!

This is your day,
Be honest and repent as you pray,
You shall always be happy and gay!